JOURNAL JOY, LLC

Copyright © 2020 Journal Joy, LLC
Printed in the United States of America
Website: www.thejournaljoy.com
Email: Amiyra@thatmommyjoy.com

ISBN: 978-1-7361688-0-6

All Rights Reserved. No part of this book may be reproduced, transmitted, or used in any matter without the written authorization of the author, with the exception of quotations in a book review.

This Journal Belongs to:

_____

I am Brilliant

I am Smart

I am Bold

I am a Daughter

I am Kind

I am fun

I am fair

I am a friend

I am Driven

I am Motivated

I am Energetic

I am Silly

_____

_____

_____

_____

_____

_____

_____

_____

_____

I am Remarkable

I am Cool

I am Interesting

I am a Trailblazer

_____

_____

_____

_____

_____

_____

_____

_____

_____

I am Innovative

I am a Dancer

I am Brave

I am Strong

I am Honest

I am Fierce

I am Pure Joy

I Will Set Goals

I Will Stay Focused

I Wont Give Up

I Will Be an Entreprenuer

Never forget, YOU are Brilliant!!

About the Author

ASPEN S. KING

Aspen Serenity King is a dynamic 6 year old who wants all girls to believe in their brilliance. Aspen developed a love for books as a baby, which soon turned to her desire to write her own book.. Aspen wants to encourage all children to love books as much as she.

You can purchase additional books from the author at www.thejournaljoy.com

www.ingramcontent.com/pod-product-compliance
Lightning Source LLC
Chambersburg PA
CBHW042235090526
44589CB00001B/9